D0805383

Jackson County Public Library
Seymour, Indiana 47274

WITHDRAWN

Sea Dragons

Pamela McDowell

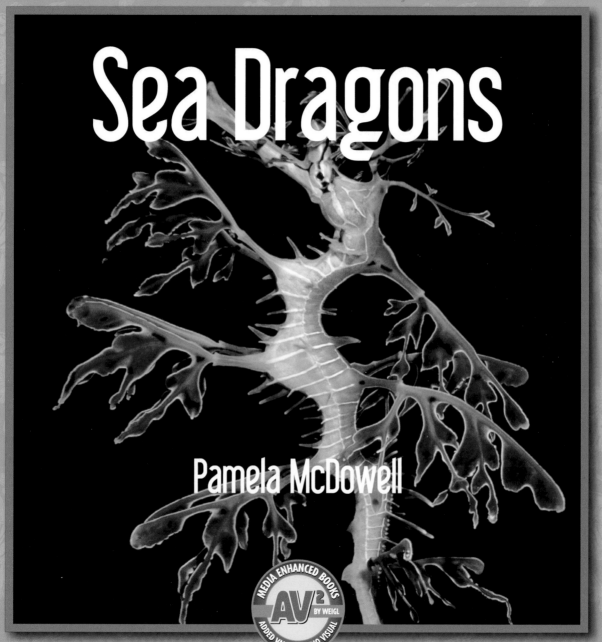

MEDIA ENHANCED BOOKS
AV2
BY WEIGL
ADDED VALUE • AUDIO VISUAL

www.av2books.com

MEDIA ENHANCED BOOKS

AV² BY WEIGL™

ADDED VALUE • AUDIO VISUAL

AV² provides enriched content that supplements and complements this book. Weigl's AV² books strive to create inspired learning and engage young minds in a total learning experience.

Your AV² Media Enhanced books come alive with...

Audio
Listen to sections of the book read aloud.

Key Words
Study vocabulary, and complete a matching word activity.

Go to **www.av2books.com**, and enter this book's unique code.

Video
Watch informative video clips.

Quizzes
Test your knowledge.

BOOK CODE

G480297

Embedded Weblinks
Gain additional information for research.

Slide Show
View images and captions, and prepare a presentation.

AV² by Weigl brings you media enhanced books that support active learning.

Try This!
Complete activities and hands-on experiments.

... and much, much more!

Published by AV² by Weigl
350 5th Avenue, 59th Floor New York, NY 10118
Website: www.av2books.com   www.weigl.com

Copyright ©2012 AV² by Weigl
All rights reserved. No part of this publication may be reproduced, stored in a retrieval system, or transmitted in any form or by any means, electronic, mechanical, photocopying, recording, or otherwise, without the prior written permission of the publisher.

Library of Congress Cataloging-in-Publication Data

McDowell, Pamela.
 Sea dragons / Pamela McDowell.
   p. cm. -- (Ocean life)
 Includes index.
 ISBN 978-1-61690-831-7 (hardcover : alk. paper) -- ISBN 978-1-61690-832-4 (softcover : alk. paper)
 1. Seadragons--Juvenile literature. I. Title.
 QL638.S9M33 2011
 597'.679--dc22

                    2010051086

Printed in the United States of America in North Mankato, Minnesota
1 2 3 4 5 6 7 8 9 0   15 14 13 12 11

052011
WEP37500

Project Coordinator: Aaron Carr
Art Director: Terry Paulhus

Weigl acknowledges Getty Images, Dreamstime, iStockphoto, and Peter Arnold as image suppliers for this title.

CONTENTS

What is a Sea Dragon?

Have you ever seen a fish that looks like seaweed? It may have been a sea dragon. A sea dragon has a long, thin body. The body looks like it is covered with leaves.

There are two kinds of sea dragons. Leafy sea dragons have large leafy parts. Weedy sea dragons have small leafy parts.

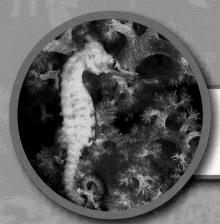

Sea dragons are related to seahorses.

Where in the World

Did you know sea dragons are only found in one place in the world? They live in the ocean near Australia. There, sea dragons hide in the seaweed that grows close to the **shore**.

Sea dragons were given their name because they look like the dragons in Chinese stories.

Sea Dragon Size

Can you imagine a dragon the size of your arm? Leafy sea dragons can grow to be 13.8 inches (35 centimeters) long. Weedy sea dragons can be up to 18 inches (45 cm) long. That is about the length of an eight-year-old child's arm.

Sea dragons are about the size of a quarter when they are born.

Hard Skin

Have you ever worn a helmet while riding a bike? Helmets have a hard shell that keeps you safe. A sea dragon is protected by hard plates that cover its whole body. These plates are bumpy and prickly. They help protect sea dragons from **predators**.

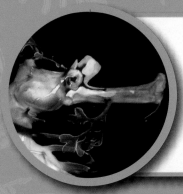

A sea dragon can look to the left with one eye and to the right with the other eye. This lets it see in all directions at the same time.

12

Can You Spot the Sea Dragon?

How does a sea dragon hide from predators?
A sea dragon's leafy parts are not used for
swimming. They help sea dragons hide.
Other fish think the sea dragon is a part
of the seaweed.

Sea dragons let their leafy
parts wave like seaweed.
This makes the sea dragon
the only animal in the world
that hides by moving.

On the Move

Have you ever paddled a canoe? A sea dragon has a clear **fin** on its back that works like a paddle. This fin pushes the sea dragon forward. A sea dragon has small fins on the side of its head that help it steer.

Sea dragons are slow swimmers. Most of the time, they float in one place. They let the **current** of the water move them.

Straw Food

Can you imagine eating all of your food through a straw? A sea dragon's mouth is shaped like a tube. It works like a straw to suck up food. A sea dragon does not have teeth. It only eats food it can swallow in one bite.

Sea dragons **prey** on sea lice. Sea lice are tiny water animals. One sea dragon can eat thousands of sea lice in a single day.

Sea Dragon Dads

Did you know that sea dragon dads carry the babies? Female sea dragons lay up to 250 eggs at one time. The female places these bright pink eggs on a patch under the male's tail. Then, he carries the eggs on his tail until they hatch. This takes about four to six weeks.

Baby sea dragons can swim within a few hours of birth. They do not need help from their parents to survive.

19

Saving Sea Dragons

What dangers do sea dragons face? People are the greatest danger to sea dragons. **Waste** from cities is dumped into the ocean. This waste harms the seaweed and other plants sea dragons need to live.

Divers used to catch sea dragons to keep as pets. This left fewer sea dragons in nature. Now, taking sea dragons from their **habitat** is against the law.

Sea Dragon Puppet

Supplies
one piece of construction paper, one piece of tissue paper the same color as the construction paper, one popsicle stick, scissors, glue, a marker

1. With an adult's help, cut out the S-shaped body of a sea dragon from the construction paper. It should be 8 to 10 inches (20 to 25 cm) long.

2. Cut 10 strips of tissue paper, about 1 inch (2.5 cm) wide and 3 to 5 inches (7.5 to 13 cm) long. These are the leafy fins of your sea dragon.

3. Put a dot of glue on the end of one of the strips of tissue paper. Attach it to the head or body of the sea dragon. Continue attaching all the strips on both sides of the sea dragon.

4. Glue the popsicle stick to the bottom of the sea dragon body to create a handle for your puppet.

5. Use a marker to draw an eye on each side of the sea dragon's head.

6. When the glue is dry, help your sea dragon swim by bobbing the puppet up and down. Does the tissue paper flutter in the air? This is how the sea dragon's leafy fins float in the ocean.

Glossary

current: the movement of water

fin: a flat flap that sticks out from the body of an animal that lives in water; used for swimming

habitat: the place where an animal naturally lives

predators: animals that hunt other animals for food

prey: to hunt an animal for food

shore: the land along the edge of a body of water

waste: something that has been thrown away or not used

Index

Log on to www.av2books.com

AV² by Weigl brings you media enhanced books that support active learning. Go to www.av2books.com, and enter the special code found on page 2 of this book. You will gain access to enriched and enhanced content that supplements and complements this book. Content includes video, audio, web links, quizzes, a slide show, and activities.

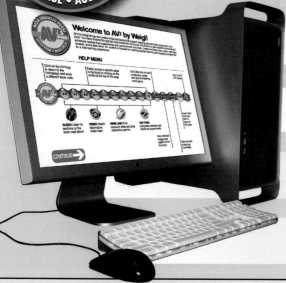

Audio
Listen to sections of the book read aloud.

Video
Watch informative video clips.

Embedded Weblinks
Gain additional information for research.

Try This!
Complete activities and hands-on experiments.

WHAT'S ONLINE?

 Try This!

Gain a better understanding of a sea dragon's size with this fun comparison activity.

Identify the benefits of a sea dragon's defensive adaptations.

Complete a fun coloring activity.

 Embedded Weblinks

Find out more information on sea dragons.

Check out myths and legends about sea dragons.

Learn more about a sea dragon's diet and nutrition.

 Video

Watch an introductory video on sea dragons.

Watch a video of a sea dragon in its natural environment.

EXTRA FEATURES

 Audio
Listen to sections of the book read aloud.

Key Words
Study vocabulary, and complete a matching word activity.

 Slide Show
View images and captions, and prepare a presentation.

 Quizzes
Test your knowledge.

AV² was built to bridge the gap between print and digital. We encourage you to tell us what you like and what you want to see in the future. Sign up to be an AV² Ambassador at www.av2books.com/ambassador.

Due to the dynamic nature of the Internet, some of the URLs and activities provided as part of AV² by Weigl may have changed or ceased to exist. AV² by Weigl accepts no responsibility for any such changes. All media enhanced books are regularly monitored to update addresses and sites in a timely manner. Contact AV² by Weigl at 1-866-649-3445 or av2books@weigl.com with any questions, comments, or feedback.

APR 2 0 2012